# Hidden Power of Music

Joe R. Eagleman, PhD

# CONTENTS

# Chapter 1: Introduction: The Power Behind the Sound

Music is far more than melody and rhythm—it is one of the most powerful yet overlooked forces in human life. We hear it in the hum of nature, the chants of ancient rituals, the pulse of drums in a parade, or the soft piano piece drifting through a quiet room. While music often entertains us, lifts our spirits, or keeps us company during mundane tasks, its full power extends far beyond enjoyment. Music has the capacity to change our brains, heal our hearts, and shape the way we relate to the world and to ourselves. The benefits of music go largely unnoticed, yet they are always at work, woven into the fabric of our daily experiences.

What if the right song could help you concentrate better at work? What if the music you listened to could reduce your anxiety, help you sleep more deeply, or even lessen physical pain? What if listening to—or making—music could enhance your memory, foster empathy, or strengthen your immune system? These are not merely theoretical ideas or wishful thinking; they are backed by a growing body of scientific research and real-world applications. The relationship between music and human well-being is rich, complex, and still being discovered. This book sets out to explore the lesser-known, yet truly transformative benefits of music.

Across cultures and history, music has served sacred and social functions. Ancient civilizations used music in ceremonies to bring rain, heal the sick, or honor the dead. In many traditions, songs were—and still are—vehicles for storytelling, education, and preserving wisdom. Today, music remains central in celebrations, worship, therapy, education, and entertainment. But modern science now confirms what these ancient practices long suggested: music influences the brain and body in measurable, meaningful ways. It lights up more parts of the brain than almost any other human activity. It can lower blood pressure, ease depression, and accelerate learning. Even people with advanced dementia can suddenly recall long-forgotten memories when they hear a familiar tune.

**Hidden Power of Music** is a book about discovering how this everyday art form can become a tool for personal growth, healing, creativity, and deeper connection. You do not need to be a musician or music scholar to understand or enjoy these benefits. Whether you play an instrument, sing in the shower, or just enjoy listening to your favorite playlists, this book will show you how music already plays a role in your well-being—and how you can engage with it more intentionally to enrich your life.

Each of the chapters that follow focuses on a unique and often surprising way that music supports human health, happiness, and connection. You will learn how music affects your brain and body, how it can enhance your learning and productivity, and how it supports emotional resilience and mental health. You'll read about its role in childhood development, aging, language learning, and even spiritual practice. The book also provides practical ideas and real-world examples for how to harness music's power—whether you're seeking better focus, deeper sleep, stress relief, or simply more joy.

In a world that often feels noisy, fast-paced, and disconnected, music offers a rare space for stillness, reflection, and unity. It speaks when words fail. It comforts when we are lonely. It energizes when we are tired. And it connects us—across differences, across generations, and even across time. As we explore the hidden benefits of music, my hope is that you will come to see music not just as something you enjoy, but as something you can *use*—as a partner in your health, your creativity, your relationships, and your journey toward a more fulfilling life.

So let us begin this exploration together. Open your ears, open your heart, and prepare to discover the remarkable, often unseen ways that music is already working wonders in your world.

# Chapter 2: Music and the Brain

If you could look inside your brain while listening to music, you would witness an incredible light show of activity. Few things stimulate the human brain as broadly and deeply as music. Unlike most stimuli, which engage specific areas of the brain, music lights up nearly every region—auditory, emotional, motor, and even memory-related areas all respond in synchrony. This widespread activation makes music not only a unique sensory experience but also a powerful tool for cognitive enhancement, healing, and emotional regulation.

At the core of music's effect on the brain is the auditory cortex, responsible for processing sound. But music doesn't stop there—it recruits the hippocampus (associated with memory), the amygdala (emotions), the prefrontal cortex (decision-making), and the cerebellum (coordination and rhythm). This interconnected response explains why music is so emotionally powerful, why it can stir up old memories, and why it can literally move us—prompting spontaneous toe-tapping or dancing. The brain recognizes patterns in melody and rhythm and often responds with pleasure, releasing dopamine, a neurotransmitter associated with motivation and reward.

Studies using brain imaging have revealed that trained musicians have enhanced connectivity between the two hemispheres of the brain, and they often show superior verbal memory and spatial reasoning skills. Even short-term music instruction has been shown to boost language development in children and increase attention span. This suggests that musical training isn't just about learning to play an instrument—it actually rewires the brain to function more efficiently across many domains.

Music also has remarkable effects on neuroplasticity—the brain's ability to adapt and form new connections. This is particularly significant in rehabilitation settings. Stroke patients who engage in music therapy, for example, often recover speech and motor skills more rapidly than those who do not. Music stimulates alternate neural pathways, allowing the brain to work around damaged areas. In cases of Parkinson's disease and other neurological disorders, rhythmic music has been used successfully to improve gait and coordination. Simply put, music gives the brain a rhythm to follow when it can't find one on its own.

Perhaps even more fascinating is music's role in memory retention and recall. People with Alzheimer's disease or other forms of dementia can often remember lyrics and melodies long after they've forgotten names or faces. This phenomenon has led to the rise of "music memory" programs in elder care, where personalized playlists can unlock moments of clarity, calm agitation, and restore a sense of identity. Music's link to memory is rooted in the brain's limbic system—where emotion and memory are closely tied. A song from one's youth doesn't just remind them of the past—it can momentarily *transport* them back to it.

Moreover, music enhances focus and productivity in both academic and workplace settings. When used strategically—especially instrumental or ambient music—it can help maintain concentration, reduce mental fatigue, and increase the retention of new information. The rhythmic elements of music can serve as a mental metronome, helping listeners stay on task. This is why many people find that certain types of music help them study, write, or engage in complex thinking.

It is important, however, to recognize that not all music affects the brain in the same way. Individual preferences, cultural background, and the task at hand all influence how beneficial music can be. For example, while classical or ambient music may enhance concentration, lyrics can be distracting during language-heavy tasks. The key is intentional listening—choosing the right music for the right moment, and being mindful of how it affects your thoughts and emotions.

Music is not just heard by the brain—it is *felt* by it. It synchronizes with our neural rhythms, stirs our emotions, and strengthens our cognition. Understanding the deep connection between music and the brain opens the door to using music not only as a form of expression or entertainment, but as a cognitive enhancer, a therapeutic agent, and a source of lifelong learning. Whether you're a student, a working professional, a parent, or a retiree, the sounds you surround yourself with can shape your mental sharpness and emotional well-being in surprising and powerful ways.

# Chapter 3: Music as Emotional Medicine

Long before therapists offered treatment plans and psychologists defined diagnoses, music served as humanity's earliest form of emotional therapy. Whether in moments of celebration or sorrow, music has been there—to lift our spirits, soothe our grief, stir our courage, and calm our nerves. Today, science has begun to explain what people have long intuited: music has a profound ability to regulate and heal our emotions. It is not merely a passive experience, but an active agent of emotional transformation.

At the heart of music's emotional power is its ability to mirror and modulate our inner states. A slow, gentle melody can slow the heart rate, lower blood pressure, and induce a sense of calm, while an upbeat, rhythmic song can energize us and elevate mood. Music activates the brain's limbic system—the same area responsible for emotions—and influences the release of key neurochemicals such as dopamine, serotonin, oxytocin, and even endorphins. These chemicals are directly linked to feelings of pleasure, bonding, and well-being. That's why a favorite song can produce a feeling of joy almost instantly, even during a difficult day.

Music therapy is now an established form of treatment for emotional and psychological conditions such as depression, anxiety, trauma, and even PTSD. In clinical settings, patients often engage with music through listening, songwriting, or improvisation. The goal is not just to entertain, but to unlock emotions that may be difficult to access through words alone. For individuals who have experienced trauma, music offers a nonverbal path to expression and healing. It provides a safe emotional container—structured and soothing—within which powerful feelings can be explored and released.

One remarkable aspect of music is its dual role: it can reflect your mood and also change it. For instance, when someone is grieving, a sad song might validate their emotions and make them feel understood. Paradoxically, this can be incredibly comforting. But music also has the ability to shift a person's emotional state—turning sadness into reflection, or anxiety into relaxation. Unlike drugs or stimulants, music doesn't force a mood—it gently invites the mind and body to align with a healthier emotional rhythm.

In daily life, many people turn to music instinctively for emotional regulation, often without realizing it. We play soft music to unwind after work, energetic tracks to get motivated for a workout, or nostalgic songs when we miss someone. These choices are not accidental; they are part of an unconscious emotional toolkit. When we become more intentional about our musical choices, this toolkit becomes a powerful form of emotional self-care.

Music also fosters emotional intelligence. Through lyrics, tone, and musical structure, it teaches us to identify and understand emotions—our own and those of others. Songs tell stories of love, loss, hope, anger, and triumph. They give voice to emotions we might struggle to articulate, and by doing so, they help us feel less alone. For adolescents especially, music becomes a critical outlet—a soundtrack for self-discovery and emotional development.

Importantly, music is also a social emotional bridge. Think of how a shared song can bond a couple, unite a crowd at a concert, or console strangers at a memorial service. Music has a unique power to create emotional resonance between people, fostering empathy and shared humanity. It speaks to something deep within us that words often cannot reach.

Even in the most fragile emotional states—such as after the loss of a loved one or during a mental health crisis—music can offer presence. It may not fix pain, but it can accompany it, soften it, and sometimes even transform it. In moments of deep solitude or suffering, a single song can feel like a friend.

As we begin to understand the biological and psychological mechanisms behind music's emotional influence, we can start using it more mindfully in our lives. Whether it's crafting a playlist to calm anxiety, singing as a form of release, or listening to lyrics that express your innermost feelings, music can be a daily dose of emotional medicine. And unlike most medicines, it is side-effect-free, accessible, and often joyfully received.

Music won't erase life's difficulties, but it can help us carry them with more grace. It can offer moments of relief, strength, and perspective in the emotional storms we all face. When we listen with intention and openness, music becomes more than background noise—it becomes a balm for the soul, a stabilizer for the heart, and a faithful companion in the journey of emotional wellness.

# Chapter 4: Boosting Academic Performance

Can music make you smarter? It's a question that has sparked both scientific curiosity and popular myths, most notably the widely circulated idea of the "Mozart Effect." While the notion that simply listening to classical music will instantly boost your IQ has been largely debunked or misinterpreted, the connection between music and enhanced academic performance is very real—and far more nuanced. Music doesn't just entertain the mind; it shapes how the mind works, especially in developing brains. When used intentionally, music can sharpen memory, strengthen focus, and even accelerate learning in academic environments.

Children who engage in music education—whether through learning an instrument, singing, or reading music—often demonstrate stronger cognitive skills than their peers. Studies have shown that students involved in music programs tend to perform better in subjects like math, reading, and language. Why? Because music reinforces many of the same brain functions used in academic learning. Reading music, for example, involves decoding symbols and translating them into action, a skill closely tied to literacy. Playing an instrument requires fine motor coordination, spatial reasoning, timing, and memory—all critical areas of brain development that transfer into other domains.

Rhythm and structure in music also support pattern recognition, which is essential in math. The understanding of musical timing, fractions in measures, and sequences in melodies can help students grasp mathematical concepts more intuitively. In fact, some educators have incorporated music-based exercises into math lessons to make abstract concepts more concrete and enjoyable. Similarly, learning songs with complex lyrics or singing in multiple languages has been shown to aid vocabulary acquisition and reading comprehension, especially in early education.

Beyond intellectual benefits, music enhances learning by improving concentration and creating a more emotionally engaging environment. Classrooms that incorporate music often report higher student participation and retention. Soft background music, when chosen carefully, can improve focus during study sessions or independent work. It helps reduce environmental distractions and creates a steady auditory atmosphere that supports sustained attention. For students with ADHD or other attention-related challenges, rhythmic or instrumental music can serve as an organizing force for the mind, helping to maintain mental clarity and reduce impulsivity.

Memory is another area where music shines as a learning tool. Have you ever noticed how easy it is to remember a song from childhood, even decades later? That's because music embeds information in a multisensory package. When facts or lessons are set to music—like the alphabet song, state capitals chants, or math rhymes—they are encoded more deeply and retrieved more easily. Teachers often use musical mnemonics to help students retain difficult concepts or sequences. The melody acts as a mental cue, triggering recall even under stress.

For older students and adults, music can still serve as an academic ally. Background music, especially instrumental genres such as classical, jazz, or ambient soundscapes, can enhance mental stamina during long study periods. It provides a steady backdrop that reduces boredom, minimizes distraction, and helps students enter a state of focused flow. However, it's important to choose the right type of music—songs with lyrics can interfere with reading or writing tasks, while high-tempo music may overstimulate. Finding the right balance takes experimentation, but once discovered, it can become a powerful habit.

Music also plays a role in emotional motivation, which is key to academic success. Studying, especially under pressure, can become a grind. But music adds color, emotion, and rhythm to the experience. A motivating playlist before a test can energize the mind and reduce anxiety. A calming piece before sleep can aid mental recovery. In this way, music supports not just the brain, but the whole learner—emotionally, mentally, and physiologically.

In school systems around the world, budget cuts often put music education on the chopping block. Ironically, eliminating music from curricula removes one of the most effective tools we have for enhancing student performance. Music is not a luxury or an extracurricular "bonus"—it is a deeply integrated form of learning that engages the brain on multiple levels. When music is treated as an essential element of education rather than an optional enrichment, students benefit across all areas of academic life.

As research continues to unfold, one thing remains clear: music nurtures minds in ways traditional education alone cannot. From improving memory and attention to fostering creativity and confidence, the hidden benefits of music in academic settings are both vast and vital. Whether you're a student, teacher, or lifelong learner, bringing music into your learning routine could be the key to unlocking deeper focus, better retention, and a more enjoyable path to success.

# Chapter 5: Physical Health and Healing Sounds

The idea that music can influence physical health may seem surprising at first, but evidence from both modern science and ancient healing traditions tells us otherwise. Music doesn't just affect how we *feel* emotionally—it can also impact how we *function* physically. From regulating heart rate and blood pressure to aiding in pain management and immune support, music has a direct line to the body's physiological systems. It is one of the few interventions that requires no prescription, has virtually no side effects, and is available to everyone, anytime, anywhere.

One of music's most immediate effects on the body is its ability to alter heart rate and breathing. Slow, gentle music—such as classical adagios, nature-inspired compositions, or soft instrumental tracks—can signal the autonomic nervous system to relax. This shift activates the parasympathetic branch, often referred to as the "rest and digest" mode, reducing cortisol (the stress hormone), slowing the pulse, and encouraging deeper, more rhythmic breathing. In contrast, upbeat music can stimulate the sympathetic nervous system, increasing alertness and providing a natural energy boost. In both cases, music helps synchronize internal rhythms, bringing the body into greater physiological balance.

Blood pressure, often influenced by stress, is another health marker music can help regulate. In studies, patients who listened to calming music regularly experienced modest but consistent reductions in both systolic and diastolic pressure. Music's ability to calm the mind and relax the body may rival, in some cases, the effects of meditation or deep breathing exercises. Some hospitals now use music as part of pre-operative preparation to reduce patient anxiety and stabilize vital signs before surgery.

Perhaps one of the most fascinating and well-documented physical benefits of music is its role in **pain management**. Listening to music has been shown to reduce the perception of pain in patients undergoing surgery, childbirth, or chronic illness treatments such as chemotherapy. This works partly through distraction—music draws the mind away from discomfort—but also through more complex biochemical mechanisms. Music can stimulate the release of endorphins, the body's natural painkillers, and reduce the intensity of pain signals sent to the brain. In clinical environments, music therapy is often used in conjunction with medication to lower dosage needs and improve patient comfort.

Beyond clinical care, music is increasingly used in **rehabilitation and physical therapy** settings. Rhythmic auditory stimulation—using beat-based music—can help stroke survivors relearn how to walk, improving their balance and gait. Parkinson's patients, who often struggle with movement and coordination, benefit from rhythmic music that provides external timing cues for motion. Even people recovering from surgery or injury report greater motivation and better results when exercising with carefully selected music. In this way, music doesn't just relax the body—it can also help retrain and restore it.

There is also growing evidence that **music supports immune function**. Stress, especially when chronic, weakens the immune system, making the body more susceptible to illness. Music that reduces anxiety and promotes relaxation indirectly boosts immunity by lowering stress hormones. Some studies have measured increases in immunoglobulin A—an important antibody for immune defense—after participants listened to soothing music. While music may not replace medical treatments, it can enhance the body's natural defenses and improve overall resilience.

Sleep, another pillar of good health, is deeply influenced by music. While we'll explore this more fully in a future chapter it's worth noting here that music's ability to lower stress, reduce racing thoughts, and create a peaceful environment plays a crucial role in sleep quality and physical restoration. Poor sleep affects everything from metabolism to cardiovascular health, so music's indirect benefits on sleep have widespread implications for physical well-being.

One of the most beautiful aspects of music's healing power is its accessibility. You don't need specialized equipment or training to benefit—just your ears and a willingness to listen. Whether you play relaxing music during a bubble bath, walk to the rhythm of your favorite song, or use a calming playlist during a medical procedure, music becomes a form of self-care that empowers you to participate in your own healing.

In hospitals, hospices, physical therapy clinics, and even birthing centers, music is quietly transforming the way we approach health. It brings comfort in moments of fear, strength during recovery, and calm amidst chaos. As science continues to document its effects, the medical community is beginning to treat music not as a luxury but as a legitimate part of integrated care. And for those of us outside clinical settings, music remains a powerful, portable ally in our journey toward better physical health.

# Chapter 6: Sleep and Soothing Sounds

Sleep is essential for mental clarity, emotional balance, physical restoration, and overall well-being. Yet in today's fast-paced, overstimulated world, restful sleep has become elusive for millions. Stress, screen time, anxiety, and lifestyle disruptions all interfere with the body's natural rhythms. While medications and supplements offer temporary fixes, music presents a gentle, natural, and lasting solution. The right kinds of sound can act like a lullaby for the adult brain—soothing the nervous system, slowing the heart rate, quieting the mind, and creating a tranquil atmosphere conducive to deep, restorative sleep.

Research has shown that listening to calming music before bed can significantly improve both the quality and quantity of sleep. In fact, studies reveal that people who integrate relaxing music into their nighttime routine fall asleep faster, wake up less frequently, and experience more restful sleep cycles. This is largely due to the way music interacts with the autonomic nervous system, the part of the body responsible for regulating involuntary functions like breathing, heart rate, and digestion. Soothing music helps shift the body into its parasympathetic "rest and repair" mode, reducing tension and promoting physiological calm.

Music also acts as a powerful cue for the brain, signaling that it's time to wind down. When paired consistently with a nightly ritual—such as dimming the lights, putting away devices, or practicing deep breathing—music becomes associated with sleep in the brain's memory system. Over time, even a few minutes of peaceful sound can prompt a relaxation response, making the transition from wakefulness to sleep much smoother. This kind of conditioned response can be especially helpful for people with insomnia or racing thoughts.

The most effective sleep-inducing music tends to be instrumental, slow in tempo (around 60–80 beats per minute), and free from sudden changes in volume or rhythm. Genres such as ambient, classical, soft jazz, or gentle acoustic music are particularly effective. Nature sounds blended with subtle melodies—like ocean waves, rain, or rustling leaves—also help create a calming soundscape. The key is consistency and simplicity. Music should not demand attention, but instead gently occupy the mind just enough to block intrusive thoughts and mental chatter.

Sleep disorders such as insomnia, restless leg syndrome, and even nightmares can all be alleviated, in part, through the use of music. Hospitals and sleep clinics are increasingly integrating music therapy as a complementary treatment, especially for patients who prefer to avoid pharmaceuticals. In elderly care homes, bedtime music has improved sleep patterns in patients with dementia and reduced the need for sleep medications. For children and teens, lullaby-style music or gentle nighttime playlists can replace overstimulating screen use, helping young people fall asleep more easily.

Beyond simply helping us fall asleep, music can improve the *quality* of sleep. Studies using brainwave monitoring have shown that music can increase time spent in slow-wave sleep—the deepest, most restorative phase of the sleep cycle, which is critical for healing, memory consolidation, and immune function. Even people who claim to be "light sleepers" have shown better outcomes when relaxing music is part of their bedtime routine.

It's also worth noting that nighttime listening doesn't require expensive equipment or complicated setups. A simple pair of comfortable earbuds or a small speaker placed near the bed can transform the sleep environment. Some people even use wearable headbands or pillow speakers designed for side-sleepers. The goal is to make the experience seamless and relaxing, free of distractions.

In a society that increasingly values productivity over rest, music invites us to reclaim the importance of stillness. It encourages the body and mind to let go, surrendering to the deep healing that only sleep can provide. By creating a sonic environment that is soothing and predictable, we send our brain a clear message: it is safe to rest, time to heal, and okay to drift away.

Incorporating music into your sleep hygiene is a simple yet transformative habit. Whether it's a short playlist of favorite soft tunes, an ambient album that plays quietly in the background, or a custom mix of nature sounds and calming chords, music can help you recover the rest your body has been craving. Over time, you may find that music doesn't just help you sleep—it helps you awaken refreshed, centered, and ready to face the day with clarity and calm.

# Chapter 7: Music and Memory in Aging

Aging brings many changes, some welcome, others more difficult. Among the most feared aspects of growing older is memory loss—the slow fading of names, faces, experiences, and even one's sense of self. But while the aging brain undergoes natural changes, music has emerged as a powerful ally in helping older adults maintain cognitive function and preserve cherished memories. Music, in many cases, becomes the bridge between past and present, reconnecting individuals to their identity, their history, and their loved ones.

One of the most striking discoveries in recent neuroscience is that musical memory often outlasts other types of memory. People with Alzheimer's disease or dementia may forget their family members' names or what they had for breakfast, yet they can recall—and sing—entire songs from their youth. This is because the parts of the brain responsible for musical memory and processing are among the last to be affected by neurodegenerative diseases. These areas, including the auditory cortex and the medial prefrontal cortex, retain function even in the advanced stages of cognitive decline.

Music is more than just a memory trigger; it's a **memory anchor**. When an individual hears a song tied to a particular time in life—a high school dance, a wedding, a favorite road trip—the brain retrieves not just the tune, but the emotions, smells, conversations, and details surrounding that moment. This emotional richness makes music a deeply effective tool for stimulating long-term memory. In dementia care, personalized playlists featuring songs from a person's youth are increasingly being used to evoke memories and reduce agitation. The results are often dramatic—bringing light to the eyes, movement to the body, and even language to lips that had been silent.

Beyond memory recall, music supports **cognitive engagement**. Learning a new instrument, even later in life, strengthens attention, processing speed, and executive function. Musical training encourages multitasking and pattern recognition—skills that help keep the brain agile. Seniors who participate in choirs, drumming circles, or music appreciation classes often show improvements not only in memory, but also in mood, social connection, and overall life satisfaction.

Social isolation is another challenge many older adults face, especially in care facilities or after the loss of a partner. Music naturally brings people together. Whether through group singing, dancing, or simply sharing favorite songs, it creates an avenue for connection and conversation. Studies have found that older adults who engage in group music activities report reduced loneliness and increased emotional well-being. These social interactions are vital for mental health and have even been linked to longer lifespans.

Music can also be a form of **emotional regulation** during times of grief or transition. The loss of independence, the passing of friends or spouses, and the changes in one's physical body can bring sadness and frustration. But music has a unique way of offering comfort without demanding words. A familiar hymn, a soothing instrumental piece, or a joyful folk song can validate emotions, offer peace, and shift focus from loss to gratitude. It helps the aging individual find a sense of continuity—something stable and familiar in a changing world.

Technology has made accessing music easier than ever for seniors. With the help of family members or caregivers, personalized playlists can be created using streaming services or portable devices. Programs like "Music & Memory" have provided thousands of seniors in care homes with access to customized music that revives long-lost memories and enhances quality of life. Even simple tools—like a CD player or old record collection—can open doors to the past and reinvigorate the present.

Importantly, music gives older adults agency. Choosing what to listen to, engaging with the rhythm, singing along, or sharing stories about favorite songs allows them to express who they are. In a stage of life where so much may feel beyond their control, music offers choice, identity, and joy. It restores dignity and reminds them—and their loved ones—that the person inside is still very much present.

As we consider the challenges of aging, we must also recognize the opportunities. Music is one of the most accessible, effective, and meaningful tools for supporting cognitive and emotional health in later life. Whether used as a memory prompt, a form of therapy, a social connector, or simply a source of comfort, music brings the past alive and keeps the mind engaged. For anyone growing older—or caring for someone who is—music can be one of the most powerful gifts we offer: a soundtrack for dignity, vitality, and treasured memories.

# Chapter 8: Building Social Bonds Through Music

From the beating of drums in tribal ceremonies to the synchronized chants of protestors, music has always had a social heartbeat. It doesn't just live within individuals—it thrives between them. Across all cultures and times, music has served as a powerful force for connection, helping people feel a sense of belonging, shared identity, and emotional resonance. Whether in choirs, concerts, families, or friend groups, music builds bridges—between generations, across cultures, and through emotional divides. Its power to connect is perhaps one of its most profound and enduring benefits.

Group music-making—such as singing in a choir, clapping to a rhythm, or dancing in unison—fosters a sense of unity and cooperation. Research has shown that when people make music together, their heart rates and brain waves often begin to synchronize. This phenomenon, known as **entrainment**, creates a physical and emotional sense of "being in sync" with others. It's why singing with a group or dancing at a wedding can produce a feeling of euphoria and togetherness. In fact, studies suggest that people who engage in shared musical activities develop increased trust, empathy, and cooperation—even among strangers.

Music also helps form **cultural and community identity**. National anthems, folk songs, spirituals, and protest music give voice to collective experiences. These songs often become emotional touchstones for entire populations—preserving stories, values, and history in a way that books alone cannot. For example, during times of oppression or struggle, music has served as a quiet (or loud) form of resistance and resilience. In the American civil rights movement, songs like *We Shall Overcome* weren't just melodies—they were unifying calls to hope and courage. Around the world, music continues to play a vital role in community healing and collective memory.

Families, too, are bonded by music. A parent singing to a child, siblings learning instruments together, or families dancing in the living room all create emotional memories that last far beyond the moment. These shared musical experiences become part of a family's story, reinforcing love and unity. Even simple rituals, like listening to a favorite song together on car rides, help establish emotional connection and create a sense of continuity and home.

In romantic relationships, music often plays a defining role. Couples commonly have "our song"—a piece of music tied to their story, evoking intimacy and nostalgia. Music can express affection, deepen emotional communication, and even help partners navigate conflict. Listening to or sharing music that reflects one's inner world can be a safe way to express difficult feelings. It creates a kind of emotional shorthand that words sometimes can't reach.

For people who feel isolated or lonely—especially in our increasingly digital world—music offers a path to **social reconnection**. Online communities have formed around shared musical tastes, fan groups, virtual choirs, and live-streamed concerts. In care homes or hospitals, music programs have brought together patients and caregivers, residents and volunteers, forging relationships where conversation may be difficult but rhythm can still be shared. Even brief moments of shared listening can produce lasting feelings of inclusion and connection.

Interestingly, playing or singing in a group releases oxytocin, the same hormone associated with bonding between mother and child or between close companions. This biological response supports what many already know intuitively: music brings us closer. Whether it's a campfire song or a church hymn, music offers an emotional glue that strengthens human connection.

Children and adolescents, in particular, use music as a key tool for social identity and group belonging. Peer groups often form around musical tastes, and favorite songs become soundtracks to teenage friendships, relationships, and rites of passage. Music helps young people feel seen, heard, and understood. It also teaches them how to collaborate, listen, and express themselves—all essential social skills.

Even across cultural and linguistic barriers, music can connect people who might otherwise never relate. A smile shared over a rhythm, or a spontaneous duet between people from different backgrounds, reminds us of our shared humanity. Music transcends language, geography, and politics. It reminds us that beneath our differences, we all respond to melody, harmony, and beat.

In a time when social disconnection and loneliness are on the rise, music offers a simple, joyful, and profound antidote. Whether through group singing, communal dancing, shared playlists, or simply enjoying the same song with someone else, music helps us feel less alone. It nurtures empathy, encourages cooperation, and strengthens our ties to others.

Ultimately, music is not just something we hear—it's something we *share*. And in that shared experience lies one of its greatest hidden benefits: the ability to draw us closer, make us feel understood, and remind us that we are all part of something larger than ourselves.

# Chapter 9: Music and Language Learning

Language and music share more than just sound—they share a deep neurological and cognitive connection that makes music an incredibly effective tool for language learning. Whether it's a child picking up their first words, a student tackling a foreign language, or an adult working to improve pronunciation and fluency, music can accelerate and deepen the process of acquiring and retaining new languages. This hidden benefit of music taps into the brain's natural ability to recognize patterns, rhythms, and melodies, which are essential components of both music and language.

At its core, language is rhythmic and melodic. Every spoken language has its unique cadence, intonation, and stress patterns that music closely mirrors. When learners listen to songs in the target language, their brains absorb not only vocabulary and grammar but also the flow and emotional tone of the speech. Singing along encourages active engagement, helping to solidify memory through repetition and melody. This multisensory approach—combining auditory, vocal, and sometimes kinesthetic learning—makes language easier to internalize and recall.

Research has shown that children exposed to music, especially singing, develop better phonological awareness—the ability to hear and manipulate sounds within words—a foundational skill for reading and speaking. Musical training improves the brain's ability to detect subtle differences in sound frequency and timing, which is crucial for distinguishing similar phonemes in a new language. This skill helps learners improve their pronunciation and listening comprehension, making their speech more natural and their understanding more accurate.

Moreover, music provides a joyful and motivating context for language practice. Singing catchy tunes or rapping rhymes makes learning feel less like a chore and more like play. Songs often repeat key vocabulary and phrases, reinforcing language patterns without learners even realizing they are studying. The emotional connection to music also aids memory—people are more likely to remember words and phrases that evoke feelings or are tied to enjoyable experiences.

Language learning through music is not just about memorization; it also helps learners understand cultural nuances embedded in language. Folk songs, traditional ballads, and popular hits reflect the values, humor, history, and social customs of a culture. By engaging with music in the target language, learners gain insights into cultural context, improving their ability to communicate authentically and respectfully.

For bilingual or multilingual individuals, music can serve as a bridge between languages, facilitating code-switching and easing transitions between different linguistic environments. Singing in multiple languages has been shown to enhance cognitive flexibility and executive control, helping the brain manage multiple language systems more effectively.

In classrooms, teachers have increasingly incorporated music-based activities to support language acquisition. From singing alphabet songs and chants to creating original lyrics, music enriches the learning environment. Technology has further expanded this benefit, with language apps, online videos, and streaming services offering countless musical resources in a variety of languages.

Adult learners, too, can benefit immensely from music. Whether learning a language for travel, work, or personal growth, music offers a low-pressure, enjoyable way to practice. Listening to popular songs, singing karaoke, or even writing one's own lyrics helps build confidence and breaks down barriers often caused by fear of making mistakes.

Ultimately, music's role in language learning reveals its extraordinary power to connect mind, body, and culture. It transforms abstract vocabulary into memorable melodies and dry grammar rules into rhythmic patterns that stick. By harnessing the natural bond between music and language, learners at any age can open doors to new worlds of communication and cultural understanding.

# Chapter 10: Productivity and Performance

In our busy, distraction-filled world, maintaining focus and maximizing productivity can feel like a constant challenge. Yet, music offers a powerful tool to enhance both mental performance and work efficiency. Whether in an office, studio, gym, or workshop, the right kind of music can sharpen attention, reduce fatigue, and boost motivation—transforming mundane tasks into energized, focused sessions. The hidden benefits of music extend far beyond relaxation and enjoyment; they include tangible improvements in how we work and perform.

One of the key ways music improves productivity is through its ability to influence **mood and motivation**. Upbeat, rhythmic music can energize the listener, triggering the release of dopamine, a neurotransmitter associated with pleasure and reward. This chemical boost elevates mood and increases willingness to tackle challenging tasks. Conversely, calm, instrumental music can help reduce stress and anxiety, creating a mental environment conducive to sustained concentration. The choice of music depends on the type of task and the individual's preferences, but when matched correctly, music can be a powerful productivity enhancer.

Research shows that music can improve **focus and attention** by masking distracting background noise, especially in noisy or open workspaces. This "auditory shield" effect allows the brain to concentrate more fully on the task at hand. For repetitive or routine activities— such as data entry, assembly line work, or household chores—music adds a pleasurable rhythm that reduces boredom and mental fatigue, enabling workers to maintain productivity longer.

In creative professions, music can stimulate **divergent thinking**, the ability to generate new ideas and see problems from fresh perspectives. Certain genres—such as classical, jazz, or ambient electronic—promote a relaxed but alert mental state, often referred to as the "flow state," where creative insight flows more freely. Musicians, writers, designers, and artists frequently report that music helps them enter this immersive zone, where distractions fade and ideas take shape.

Music's effect on **time perception** also plays a role in productivity. When working with music, time often seems to pass more quickly, making long or tedious tasks feel less burdensome. This can be especially helpful during extended periods of work or study, helping maintain motivation and reducing procrastination.

However, it's important to note that not all music is equally beneficial for productivity. Lyrics can be distracting during language-heavy tasks like writing or reading, as the brain struggles to process competing verbal input. Similarly, music with irregular rhythms or sudden changes in volume may disrupt focus rather than enhance it. Understanding your own cognitive style and experimenting with different music types can help find the ideal auditory environment.

Music also supports **physical performance**, which in turn enhances productivity in active tasks. During exercise or physically demanding work, energetic music increases endurance, reduces perceived exertion, and boosts coordination. This relationship between music and movement is so strong that athletes often rely on personalized playlists to optimize training sessions and competitions.

For teams and workplaces, shared musical experiences can enhance **group cohesion** and morale. Playing music in communal areas, celebrating milestones with songs, or creating collaborative playlists fosters a positive atmosphere and strengthens social bonds. Happy, connected teams tend to be more productive and resilient.

As remote and hybrid work becomes more common, music also offers a personal productivity anchor— helping workers create mental boundaries between "work" and "home" spaces, and signaling the start or end of focused sessions.

In essence, music is a versatile tool that, when used mindfully, can dramatically improve productivity and performance across a wide range of activities. It energizes the mind and body, shields against distractions, fosters creativity, and supports sustained effort. Integrating music into your work or study routine is a simple yet highly effective strategy to unlock hidden reserves of focus and motivation, helping you achieve your goals with greater ease and enjoyment.

# Chapter 11: Stress Reduction and Mental Health

In today's fast-paced, high-pressure world, stress has become an almost constant companion for many. Chronic stress not only diminishes quality of life but also contributes to a range of physical and mental health problems, including anxiety, depression, cardiovascular disease, and weakened immune function. While modern medicine offers various treatments, one of the most accessible and effective tools for managing stress and supporting mental health lies in something as simple as music.

Music's ability to reduce stress stems from its profound influence on both the mind and body. Listening to calming music slows the heart rate, lowers blood pressure, and reduces levels of cortisol—the body's primary stress hormone. These physiological changes promote a state of relaxation and recovery. In fact, even just a few minutes of soothing music can shift the nervous system from a state of heightened alertness or anxiety to one of calm. This shift is essential for restoring balance after stressful experiences.

Beyond the physical benefits, music engages the brain's emotional centers, offering a powerful outlet for expressing and processing feelings. Many people find that listening to or creating music allows them to release tension, sadness, or frustration in a safe, nonverbal way. Music therapy, a clinical practice that uses music interventions to address emotional and psychological needs, has been shown to be effective in treating anxiety, depression, PTSD, and other mental health conditions. Through activities such as songwriting, improvisation, or guided listening, individuals can explore and regulate their emotions more effectively.

One reason music is so effective for stress reduction is its ability to shift attention away from distressing thoughts. When the mind is caught in a cycle of worry or rumination, music provides a positive distraction that can break the loop. This redirection creates space for mindfulness and present-moment awareness, fostering a greater sense of control and emotional resilience.

Importantly, music also enhances social connection, which is vital for mental health. Group music-making or communal listening fosters feelings of belonging and support, countering loneliness and isolation—common contributors to mental health struggles. Singing in a choir or participating in drumming circles can release oxytocin, the "bonding hormone," further deepening social ties and emotional well-being.

Personal music preferences play a key role in the mental health benefits of music. What soothes one person might energize another; what calms one may evoke memories in another. Understanding one's own musical tastes and moods allows for a personalized approach to stress management. Creating playlists tailored to different emotional needs—such as relaxation, motivation, or comfort—can be a powerful self-care tool.

In clinical settings, hospitals and mental health facilities increasingly incorporate music therapy as a complementary treatment. Patients recovering from surgery, dealing with chronic pain, or managing psychiatric conditions often experience improved mood, reduced anxiety, and better coping skills when music is part of their care plan.

Music also offers a low-cost, non-invasive method for managing stress in everyday life. Whether it's a few moments of listening to peaceful piano music during a hectic workday, singing along to a favorite song on the commute, or playing an instrument to unwind, music provides an accessible way to foster mental calm and balance.

As we deepen our understanding of music's impact on the brain and body, it becomes clear that it is more than entertainment—it is a potent mental health ally. By incorporating music intentionally into daily routines, individuals can harness its healing power to reduce stress, lift mood, and enhance emotional well-being, contributing to a healthier, more balanced life.

# Chapter 12: Music and Movement

Music and movement are inseparable companions, each amplifying the power of the other. From the earliest human societies, dance and physical expression accompanied musical rhythms as a form of communication, celebration, healing, and storytelling. Today, science confirms what ancient cultures long knew: combining music and movement offers profound benefits for physical health, emotional well-being, social connection, and creative expression.

At a basic level, music naturally invites movement. The beat, tempo, and rhythm stimulate the motor regions of the brain, encouraging the body to respond. This automatic response forms the foundation for dance, exercise, and even simple gestures like tapping a foot or nodding the head. Movement to music is not only pleasurable but also physically beneficial. It enhances cardiovascular fitness, improves coordination, strengthens muscles, and boosts flexibility. Engaging in dance or rhythmic exercise accompanied by music can make physical activity more enjoyable, increasing motivation and adherence to healthy routines.

Dance, as a form of physical expression, transcends language and culture. It provides a universal way to communicate emotions, tell stories, and connect with others. For individuals of all ages and abilities, dance offers a creative outlet for self-expression, helping to release tension, process emotions, and experience joy. Studies show that dancing improves mood by releasing endorphins and reducing stress hormones, creating a natural high often referred to as the "dancer's high."

In therapeutic settings, dance and movement therapies use music to facilitate healing on physical, emotional, and psychological levels. These therapies encourage body awareness, self-esteem, and emotional release. For people recovering from trauma, dance movement therapy can reconnect mind and body, fostering a sense of safety and empowerment. Similarly, for seniors, dance classes improve balance, reduce fall risk, and stimulate cognitive function.

Group dance experiences, such as social dances, cultural ceremonies, or fitness classes, strengthen social bonds and build community. Moving in synchrony with others to shared music enhances feelings of belonging and trust. Neuroscience research has shown that synchronous movement increases cooperation and prosocial behavior, reinforcing the social fabric that music and dance help weave.

Music also enhances other forms of physical expression beyond dance. Athletes use music to synchronize movements, improve timing, and boost endurance. Performing artists, including actors and musicians, rely on music to inspire expressive gestures and emotional nuance. Even everyday gestures—smiling, clapping, or rhythmic work movements—gain energy and intention when paired with music.

Technology has expanded the ways people combine music and movement, from virtual dance classes to interactive fitness apps. This accessibility allows people around the world to experience the physical and emotional benefits of moving to music, regardless of location or ability.

In sum, the union of music and movement is a dynamic, holistic experience that nurtures body, mind, and spirit. Whether through formal dance, spontaneous gestures, or exercise routines, moving with music enhances physical health, fosters emotional release, and deepens social connection. It invites us to embody rhythm, express creativity, and celebrate the joy of being alive in motion.

# Chapter 13: Music in Rituals and Spirituality

Throughout history, music has held a sacred place in rituals and spiritual practices, serving as a bridge between the mundane and the transcendent. From ancient tribal ceremonies to modern religious services, music has been used to mark moments of transformation, communicate with the divine, and foster a sense of sacred connection. The hidden benefits of music in these contexts extend far beyond aesthetics; it shapes communal identity, deepens spiritual experience, and promotes psychological healing.

Rituals often involve repetitive sounds, chants, or hymns that create a hypnotic effect, helping participants enter altered states of consciousness. These musical elements guide the mind and body into a focused, meditative state where spiritual insight, emotional release, or collective unity can occur. Neuroscientific research reveals that such music activates brain regions linked to emotion, attention, and self-awareness, explaining why music can facilitate mystical or transcendent experiences.

In many cultures, music functions as a form of prayer or invocation, offering words and melodies to honor deities, ancestors, or the forces of nature. The act of singing or playing instruments becomes a form of devotion and surrender, allowing individuals to express gratitude, seek guidance, or release burdens. This sacred music often carries symbolic meaning—specific rhythms, scales, or modes are chosen for their spiritual significance and their power to affect the listener's inner state.

Music's role in ritual also fosters communal belonging. Shared musical participation during ceremonies strengthens social bonds and affirms collective identity. Whether through call-and-response singing, drumming circles, or communal chants, music creates a shared emotional and spiritual space where individuals feel connected to each other and to something larger than themselves. This sense of unity is a powerful antidote to loneliness and fragmentation, offering comfort and meaning.

Spiritual traditions around the world use music as a pathway for healing. Chanting, sacred songs, and instrumental music can calm the nervous system, release emotional blockages, and promote inner peace. Many people report profound healing experiences during musical rituals, finding relief from anxiety, depression, or grief. In this way, music is both a spiritual practice and a therapeutic tool.

Modern spiritual movements and mindfulness practices continue to embrace music's transformative potential. Meditation music, singing bowls, and mantra chanting have become popular methods for cultivating presence, compassion, and spiritual growth. These practices invite listeners to slow down, tune inward, and experience a deeper connection to themselves and the world around them.

Importantly, music in spirituality transcends religious boundaries. While particular traditions may have unique musical forms, the fundamental human experience of music as a gateway to the sacred is universal. People from diverse backgrounds find solace, inspiration, and transformation through musical spirituality, reflecting our shared need for connection to mystery and meaning.

In summary, music's role in rituals and spirituality reveals its profound capacity to shape consciousness, nurture community, and foster healing. It invites us to step beyond ordinary experience, touch the sacred, and find a deeper sense of belonging and purpose. Whether in ancient ceremonies or contemporary spiritual practices, music remains a vital thread weaving together the human experience of the divine.

# Chapter 14: Music and Creativity

Creativity—the ability to generate new ideas, solve problems, and express oneself uniquely—is a cornerstone of human innovation and fulfillment. Music, with its rich patterns, emotional depth, and dynamic flow, serves as a powerful catalyst for creativity across all domains. Whether in the arts, sciences, business, or daily life, music stimulates the brain's creative networks, unlocking fresh perspectives and inspiring original thought.

At its core, music engages both hemispheres of the brain, fostering integration between logical analysis and intuitive insight. Listening to or creating music activates neural pathways involved in imagination, abstract thinking, and emotional processing. This neurological stimulation primes the mind to think divergently—to make unexpected connections and explore novel possibilities. For many artists, musicians, and writers, music provides a fertile mental landscape where ideas flourish.

In practical terms, music can enhance creative problem-solving by improving mood and reducing stress, both of which are crucial for open thinking. A relaxed, positive mental state encourages risk-taking and experimentation, while a stressed or anxious mind tends to become rigid and self-critical. Playing or listening to music helps quiet the inner critic, allowing creative impulses to emerge unfiltered. The rhythm and flow of music also mirror the creative process, which often involves cycles of exploration, refinement, and breakthrough.

Music's influence on creativity extends beyond the arts. Scientists, engineers, and entrepreneurs have reported that listening to music helps them think more flexibly, generate innovative solutions, and maintain focus during complex tasks. In brainstorming sessions, background music can foster collaboration and idea exchange by creating an energizing, yet non-distracting, atmosphere. Some workplaces incorporate music strategically to boost creative output and team synergy.

Creative disciplines often use music as a direct source of inspiration. Composers draw from nature, emotions, or social issues to create pieces that express ideas beyond words. Visual artists may listen to music to evoke moods that guide their brushstrokes or color choices. Writers often use music to set the tone or rhythm of their narratives. This interplay between music and other art forms exemplifies the cross-pollination of creative energy.

Improvisation, a key aspect of musical creativity, teaches valuable lessons about spontaneity, listening, and adaptation. Jazz musicians, for example, rely on improvisation to communicate and innovate in real-time, demonstrating how creativity thrives in collaboration and flexibility. This skill translates well beyond music, encouraging people to embrace uncertainty and respond inventively to changing circumstances.

In education, integrating music into creative learning environments supports students in developing cognitive flexibility and expressive confidence. Schools that incorporate music, drama, and movement alongside traditional subjects nurture well-rounded thinkers capable of tackling challenges creatively. Music provides a joyful and motivating context for experimenting with ideas and self-expression.

On a personal level, engaging with music—whether through listening, playing, or composing—can unlock latent creativity in everyday life. It invites individuals to explore their inner worlds, express emotions, and reimagine familiar experiences. The process of creating or engaging with music becomes a journey of self-discovery and growth.

In essence, music is a gateway to the creative mind. It opens pathways for imagination, fuels emotional expression, and fosters the resilience needed to innovate. By embracing music as a tool for creativity, individuals and communities can enrich their lives, solve problems more effectively, and cultivate a deeper sense of purpose and joy.

# Chapter 15: Music and Emotional Intelligence

Emotional intelligence—the ability to recognize, understand, and manage one's own emotions while empathizing with others—is a vital skill for personal growth, relationships, and effective communication. Music plays a surprisingly powerful role in developing and enhancing emotional intelligence by deepening our awareness of feelings and teaching us how to express and regulate them. Through music, people learn to connect with their emotions in nuanced ways, cultivating empathy and emotional resilience.

At its core, music is an emotional language. It communicates joy, sorrow, tension, and release without words, allowing listeners to experience and identify complex feelings. When we listen attentively to music, our brains process emotional cues such as melody, harmony, tempo, and dynamics, which mirror the emotional contours of human experience. This sensory engagement enhances our ability to perceive subtle shifts in mood, tone, and emotional expression both in music and in real life.

Music encourages **emotional awareness** by providing a safe space to explore feelings that might be difficult to articulate otherwise. Many people find that music helps them label and understand emotions such as grief, anger, or hope, which might otherwise remain unconscious or overwhelming. For example, a melancholic song can help someone acknowledge sadness, while an uplifting melody can inspire courage and optimism. This process of emotional labeling is a foundational component of emotional intelligence.

Beyond awareness, music helps individuals practice **emotional regulation**—the ability to manage and respond to emotions appropriately. Listening to calming music can soothe anxiety or agitation, while energetic music can motivate and energize. Musicians, through the act of performing or composing, learn to channel their emotions constructively, balancing intensity and control. This practice fosters resilience, teaching that emotions are not threats but resources that can be managed skillfully.

Music also enhances **empathy**, a key aspect of emotional intelligence. By engaging with music from diverse cultures, genres, and perspectives, listeners gain insight into experiences and emotions different from their own. Storytelling songs, operas, and musical dramas often invite us into the lives of others, broadening our emotional horizons. Group music-making—such as singing in a choir or playing in an ensemble—builds shared emotional understanding and connection, reinforcing social empathy.

In educational and therapeutic settings, music is used to develop emotional intelligence in children and adults alike. Music therapy interventions support individuals in recognizing emotions, improving social skills, and coping with emotional challenges. Schools that integrate music into their curriculum report enhanced emotional and social development among students, helping them navigate interpersonal relationships more effectively.

Furthermore, music's role in emotional intelligence extends to its power in communication. Songs often express what words alone cannot, allowing people to convey emotions authentically and creatively. This expression fosters openness and vulnerability, building trust and deeper connections in personal and professional relationships.

In a world where emotional literacy is increasingly recognized as crucial for success and well-being, music offers an accessible and engaging path to growth. Whether through listening, performing, or creating, music cultivates a richer emotional life, helping individuals understand themselves and others with greater compassion and insight.

In summary, music's capacity to enhance emotional intelligence lies in its ability to connect us deeply with feelings, teach emotional regulation, and foster empathy. By embracing music as a tool for emotional development, we nurture not only our own well-being but also the quality of our relationships and communities.

# Chapter 16: Music and Mindfulness

Mindfulness—the practice of paying purposeful, nonjudgmental attention to the present moment—has gained widespread recognition for its benefits in reducing stress, improving focus, and enhancing emotional well-being. Music serves as a natural and powerful partner to mindfulness, offering a gateway to deeper presence, awareness, and inner calm. Through attentive listening or intentional music-making, individuals can cultivate mindfulness in an accessible and engaging way.

Music naturally captures attention. Its patterns, rhythms, and melodies invite the mind to focus, creating an anchor in the present moment. When practiced mindfully, listening to music involves observing sounds without judgment or distraction—simply noticing the texture of a note, the rise and fall of a phrase, or the interplay of instruments. This focused awareness helps quiet mental chatter and cultivates a sense of spaciousness in the mind, which is central to mindfulness practice.

Mindful music listening differs from passive background listening by engaging active, present-moment awareness. Instead of multitasking or zoning out, the listener intentionally attends to the music's qualities, allowing themselves to be fully immersed. This practice fosters deep relaxation and a rich sensory experience, promoting emotional balance and stress reduction. The simple act of slowing down to listen fully can reconnect individuals to a sense of peace amid life's busyness.

Creating music mindfully—whether through singing, playing an instrument, or improvising—further deepens mindfulness by engaging body, breath, and mind in coordinated awareness. Musicians must attend closely to timing, tone, and expression, which cultivates concentration and flow. This embodied mindfulness enhances self-awareness and presence, grounding individuals in their physical and emotional experience.

Many meditation and mindfulness traditions incorporate music or chanting as focal points for practice. Repetitive mantras or calming soundscapes support sustained attention and create a sonic environment conducive to deep meditation. Singing bowls, tuning forks, and other tonal instruments are often used to mark transitions in mindfulness sessions, helping practitioners settle into a centered state.

Scientific studies show that music combined with mindfulness practice can amplify benefits such as reduced anxiety, improved mood, and better sleep. Music helps regulate the nervous system by activating the parasympathetic response, fostering relaxation and resilience. For those new to mindfulness, music offers an inviting entry point that makes the practice more enjoyable and accessible.

Beyond individual benefits, mindful music listening can enhance empathy and social connection. When groups listen to music together with focused attention, they share a collective experience of presence and openness, strengthening bonds and creating a sense of unity.

In everyday life, integrating music with mindfulness encourages a more attentive and joyful engagement with the world. Whether savoring a favorite song, exploring new genres with curiosity, or using music to anchor meditation, this practice nurtures appreciation and wonder. It teaches us to listen not only to music but to life itself with greater depth and clarity.

In essence, music and mindfulness together create a harmonious path to inner calm, heightened awareness, and emotional well-being. By embracing mindful music practices, individuals can cultivate presence, reduce stress, and enrich their connection to themselves and the world around them.

# Chapter 17: Music and Healing

Music has long been recognized as a powerful force for healing—both physical and emotional. Across cultures and throughout history, it has been used in rituals, ceremonies, and therapeutic settings to promote recovery, comfort, and transformation. Modern science now confirms what ancient wisdom has known: music can stimulate the body's healing processes, alleviate pain, support mental health, and enhance quality of life.

On a physical level, music influences the nervous, endocrine, and immune systems in profound ways. Listening to soothing music has been shown to reduce the perception of pain, lower blood pressure, and decrease levels of stress hormones such as cortisol. These physiological effects create an environment conducive to healing by calming the body's fight-or-flight response and promoting relaxation. In hospitals, music therapy is increasingly used to ease anxiety before surgeries, reduce post-operative pain, and improve recovery outcomes.

Music also facilitates healing on an emotional and psychological level. Traumatic experiences, grief, and chronic illness often leave emotional wounds that can be difficult to express through words alone. Music provides a safe, nonverbal outlet for processing complex feelings, releasing tension, and finding comfort. Through improvisation, songwriting, or guided listening, individuals can explore and express emotions, fostering emotional release and resilience.

In clinical settings, music therapy—delivered by trained professionals—tailors musical interventions to meet individual needs. Techniques may include active music-making, receptive listening, or lyric analysis, all aimed at supporting cognitive, emotional, and physical healing. Patients with conditions ranging from depression and PTSD to dementia and stroke have shown improvements in mood, communication, and motor skills through music therapy.

Beyond formal therapy, music serves as a personal healing tool that individuals can use daily. Listening to favorite songs, singing, or playing instruments can provide solace during difficult times and boost overall well-being. Music's ability to evoke positive memories and emotions strengthens coping resources and fosters hope.

Culturally, music's role in healing rituals connects individuals to community and tradition. Ceremonies that incorporate music—whether through chant, drumming, or song—offer collective support and a sense of belonging, reinforcing psychological healing. These shared musical experiences remind us that healing is not only an individual journey but a communal one.

Research into music's healing potential continues to expand, revealing new applications and mechanisms. Advances in neuroscience show that music engages brain areas involved in emotion regulation, motor control, and memory, highlighting its multifaceted impact on health. This growing body of knowledge encourages healthcare providers and individuals alike to embrace music as a complementary approach to healing.

Ultimately, music's power to heal lies in its ability to engage the whole person—body, mind, and spirit. It offers comfort in pain, expression in silence, and connection in isolation. By integrating music into healing practices and everyday life, we unlock a resource that nurtures recovery, fosters resilience, and restores hope.

# Chapter 18: Music and Childhood Development

From a baby's first lullaby to the songs sung in schoolyards, music plays a vital role in childhood development. Far beyond entertainment, music profoundly shapes the cognitive, emotional, social, and physical growth of children. Its rhythms, melodies, and patterns support brain development, language acquisition, emotional regulation, and social skills, making music an indispensable part of nurturing a child's full potential.

Neurologically, music engages multiple brain regions simultaneously, including those responsible for auditory processing, motor skills, memory, and emotion. This multisensory stimulation enhances neural connectivity and plasticity, which are crucial during the formative years. Research indicates that children exposed to music education or enriched musical environments often demonstrate superior abilities in spatial reasoning, math skills, and verbal memory compared to peers without similar experiences.

Music aids language development in remarkable ways. Singing nursery rhymes, chants, and songs introduces children to vocabulary, syntax, and phonemic awareness. The rhythmic and repetitive nature of music makes it easier for young minds to absorb the sounds and structures of language. These early musical experiences lay the groundwork for literacy and effective communication.

Emotionally, music provides children with a safe outlet for expressing feelings they may not yet have the words to describe. Songs about joy, sadness, fear, or excitement help children recognize and name emotions, fostering emotional intelligence from a young age. Engaging in musical play also promotes self-regulation, helping children learn to manage impulses and develop patience.

Socially, music offers rich opportunities for interaction and cooperation. Group singing, dancing, and musical games teach children to listen to others, take turns, and work as part of a team. These shared experiences build empathy, communication skills, and a sense of belonging—foundations for healthy relationships throughout life.

Physically, music supports motor development through activities that require coordination and timing. Clapping, tapping, dancing, and playing instruments refine fine and gross motor skills while encouraging body awareness. These physical interactions with music contribute to overall health and well-being.

Music's role in childhood extends into education and therapy. Many schools incorporate music into their curricula to enhance learning and engagement. Music therapy is used to support children with developmental delays, autism spectrum disorders, and emotional challenges, demonstrating improvements in communication, social skills, and emotional regulation.

Parents and caregivers also play a critical role by introducing music early and creating a musically rich environment at home. Simple activities like singing lullabies, playing musical toys, or listening to varied genres nurture a lifelong love of music and its associated benefits.

In essence, music is a fundamental ingredient in the tapestry of childhood development. It nurtures the brain, body, and heart, fostering skills and capacities that serve children throughout their lives. By embracing music's role in early growth, families and educators can support children in becoming healthy, creative, and emotionally intelligent individuals.

# Chapter 19: Music and Mental Resilience

Mental resilience—the capacity to adapt and thrive in the face of adversity, stress, or trauma—is a vital skill in today's unpredictable world. Building resilience helps individuals recover from setbacks, maintain emotional balance, and sustain well-being during challenging times. Music, often overlooked as a tool for mental strength, plays a powerful role in fostering resilience by supporting emotional regulation, providing comfort, and enhancing coping strategies.

One of the key ways music builds mental resilience is through its ability to influence mood and emotional states. During difficult moments, listening to music that resonates emotionally can offer solace, validation, and hope. Music has the unique capacity to mirror our feelings, making us feel understood and less isolated. For example, a melancholic tune may allow for the healthy expression of sadness, while an uplifting melody can inspire courage and optimism. This emotional attunement helps individuals process their experiences constructively rather than becoming overwhelmed or stuck.

Music also supports resilience by enhancing **emotional regulation**—the ability to manage one's emotional responses effectively. Engaging with music, whether by listening, singing, or playing an instrument, can calm the nervous system, reduce anxiety, and promote relaxation. This calming effect provides a buffer against stress, helping individuals regain composure and clarity during crises. Moreover, creating music encourages mindful focus and presence, which are crucial for responding adaptively to challenges rather than reacting impulsively.

Another important aspect of music's contribution to resilience lies in its capacity to foster **positive coping mechanisms**. When faced with hardship, many people turn to music as a healthy outlet for expression and distraction. Songwriting, drumming, or simply moving to music offers ways to channel difficult emotions safely. These creative activities build a sense of mastery and control, empowering individuals to take an active role in their healing and growth. Music also facilitates social connection—a key protective factor in resilience—by bringing people together in shared experiences such as choirs, concerts, or online communities.

Research supports the role of music in resilience-building. Studies with trauma survivors, military veterans, and individuals with chronic illness have shown that music therapy can reduce symptoms of PTSD, depression, and anxiety, while increasing feelings of hope and self-efficacy. The ritual of engaging with music regularly creates structure and meaning, helping individuals find purpose even amid uncertainty.

On a neurological level, music activates brain circuits involved in reward, motivation, and emotion regulation. This engagement helps rebuild neural pathways disrupted by stress and trauma, supporting recovery and adaptive functioning. Furthermore, the rhythmic elements of music promote physiological regulation by stabilizing heart rate and breathing patterns, contributing to a sense of safety and being grounded.

Importantly, music's role in resilience is accessible to everyone, regardless of musical training or background. Even passive listening can provide mental health benefits, while active participation deepens the impact. Personalizing music choices to fit one's cultural identity, preferences, and emotional needs enhances the effectiveness of this resilience tool.

Incorporating music intentionally into daily life— through morning playlists, breaks with calming tunes, or evening wind-down rituals—can build a resilient mindset over time. Encouraging children and youth to engage with music nurtures early development of coping skills and emotional strength, laying the foundation for lifelong resilience.

In conclusion, music is a powerful ally in the cultivation of mental resilience. It nurtures emotional awareness, supports regulation, fosters connection, and inspires hope. By embracing music as a tool for resilience, individuals can navigate life's challenges with greater strength, flexibility, and optimism—transforming hardship into growth.

# Chapter 20: Creating Your Own Musical Life

Music is more than something we listen to—it's an experience we can actively shape and integrate into our daily lives. Creating your own musical life means making music a personal, meaningful part of your routine, enhancing your well-being, creativity, and connection with others. Whether you are a seasoned musician or a complete beginner, crafting a musical life tailored to your tastes and goals can unlock countless hidden benefits.

The first step in creating your musical life is cultivating **awareness and intention**. Consider what role music already plays for you and how you want it to enrich your life further. Are you seeking relaxation, motivation, emotional expression, social connection, or creative growth? Identifying your needs helps you choose the right musical activities and experiences to pursue.

Listening is the most accessible entry point. Building diverse playlists for different moods and activities—

energizing music for workouts, soothing tunes for relaxation, or inspiring melodies for creative work—allows music to support various aspects of your day. Experimenting with new genres, artists, or cultures can broaden your musical horizons and deepen your appreciation.

Beyond listening, engaging actively with music transforms it from a passive experience into a vibrant practice. Learning to sing or play an instrument—even at a basic level—cultivates mindfulness, discipline, and joy. Many adults find that starting with simple instruments like the ukulele or keyboard brings a sense of accomplishment and fun without overwhelming complexity. Group classes or online tutorials make learning accessible and social.

Creating your own music, whether through songwriting, improvisation, or digital production, opens a channel for authentic self-expression. Writing lyrics or composing melodies allows you to explore emotions and ideas that might be difficult to convey otherwise. This creative process can be deeply therapeutic, enhancing emotional intelligence and resilience.

Incorporating music into daily rituals anchors your musical life in routine. Morning sing-alongs, driving playlists, or evening wind-down sessions can mark transitions, boost mood, and foster mindfulness. Using music to accompany chores, exercise, or work can increase productivity and enjoyment.

Social connection is a vital dimension of a musical life. Participating in choirs, bands, jam sessions, or dance classes fosters community and shared joy. Music brings people together across cultures and generations, strengthening relationships and building empathy. Virtual platforms now enable global musical collaborations, expanding opportunities for connection.

Technology offers powerful tools for creating and sharing music. Apps for recording, composing, and mixing empower beginners and professionals alike to produce music from home. Online communities provide feedback, encouragement, and inspiration, making music creation a social and accessible endeavor.

Balancing music with life's demands requires flexibility and self-compassion. Your musical life can ebb and flow with changing interests, schedules, and energy levels. The key is maintaining a positive, playful attitude and honoring music as a source of pleasure and growth rather than obligation.

Ultimately, creating your own musical life is about weaving music into your identity and daily experience. It invites you to explore your voice, celebrate your creativity, and cultivate joy and connection. By making music a personal practice, you unlock its transformative power to enrich every facet of your life.

# Chapter 21: Interesting Examples of How Music Helped Someone

Music's transformative power shines brightest in the real-life stories of people whose lives were profoundly changed by it. Across the world and throughout history, countless individuals have found healing, inspiration, and hope through music. These compelling examples reveal the hidden benefits of music in ways that resonate deeply, offering encouragement and insight for anyone seeking to harness music's potential in their own life.

Consider the story of *James*, a veteran who returned home burdened by post-traumatic stress disorder (PTSD). Struggling with nightmares, anxiety, and isolation, James found it difficult to reconnect with daily life. Through a music therapy program, he began drumming in group sessions designed to rebuild trust and emotional regulation. The steady rhythms gave James a sense of control and presence, helping him manage flashbacks and reconnect with others. Over time, music became a lifeline—a way to express pain without words and to find community. His story exemplifies how music supports resilience and healing after trauma.

In another inspiring example, *Maria*, a young girl with autism, faced challenges in communication and social interaction. Traditional therapies yielded limited progress, but when her therapists introduced singing and musical games, Maria's engagement blossomed. The predictable patterns and emotional cues in music helped her connect with others and express herself more freely. Her parents witnessed her first words emerge through song, marking a breakthrough that transformed her development. Maria's experience highlights music's unique ability to reach and support neurodiverse individuals.

The renowned cellist *Yo-Yo Ma* provides a different perspective on music's power. Beyond his virtuosity, Ma has spoken about how music bridges cultural divides and fosters empathy. During collaborations with musicians from conflict zones, he observed that sharing music created bonds where words failed. These experiences reinforced his belief that music is a universal language that nurtures understanding and peace, demonstrating music's social and spiritual benefits.

On a more everyday level, *Sarah*, a busy working mother, found solace in music amid the chaos of daily life. After discovering mindfulness meditation combined with gentle music, Sarah developed a practice that reduced her anxiety and improved sleep. She also began singing in a community choir, which provided friendship and joy. Music became her personal refuge and source of strength, illustrating how integrating music into routine life enhances mental health and well-being.

Athletes also turn to music for motivation and performance. *David*, a marathon runner, credits his playlist of upbeat songs with helping him push through pain and exhaustion during races. The rhythms helped synchronize his movements, while the lyrics fueled his determination. Music became an invisible coach, illustrating how it can enhance physical endurance and mental toughness.

Historical figures such as *Ludwig van Beethoven* show music's profound emotional and psychological impact. Despite losing his hearing, Beethoven continued to compose masterpieces that expressed the depths of human emotion and resilience. His story inspires us to see music not only as a source of joy but as a powerful means to transcend adversity.

These examples—from therapeutic breakthroughs to everyday coping, from artistic triumph to social connection—underscore music's multifaceted benefits. They reveal how music can heal wounds, ignite creativity, build community, and sustain hope. Each story offers a unique lens on the hidden power of music, encouraging readers to explore and embrace music's role in their own lives.

In essence, music is more than sound; it is a force that touches hearts, changes minds, and transforms lives. The stories of those who have been helped by music invite us all to listen more deeply, participate more fully, and recognize the extraordinary potential that music holds for every human being.

# Chapter 22: How the Music of Elvis Affected Different Groups

When Elvis Presley first took the stage on national television, America collectively gasped—and then leaned in. With a rebellious swagger, velvet voice, and unorthodox moves, he became not just a singer but a seismic cultural event. Elvis was more than a performer—he was a catalyst. His music, image, and style impacted a variety of groups across society, each in different and often surprising ways.

## Teenagers: A Cultural Earthquake for the Youth

Before Elvis, there was no such thing as "teenagers" in the cultural sense. Youth were expected to become miniature adults, adopting their parents' values and tastes. But Elvis offered something completely new: a sound and persona that celebrated youthful emotion, desire, and rebellion.

Songs like *"Jailhouse Rock"*, *"All Shook Up"*, and *"Heartbreak Hotel"* pulsed with a kind of wild honesty that spoke directly to young people's experience. For many teens in the 1950s, Elvis was the first figure who made them feel understood, excited, and independent. His appearance on *The Ed Sullivan Show* in 1956, famously shot only from the waist up due to his hip movements, still reached 60 million viewers—an astounding 82.6% of the television audience.

Elvis didn't just entertain teenagers—he gave them cultural permission to have their own identity. This was the dawn of youth culture, and Presley was its first king.

## African Americans: Cultural Conduit or Cultural Thief?

Elvis' music was rooted in the sounds of Black America. He often credited his early musical inspiration to African American gospel and blues artists. He spent time in Memphis' Black neighborhoods and was known to have visited Black churches to listen and learn.

Artists like B.B. King, Sister Rosetta Tharpe, and Big Mama Thornton (whose song *"Hound Dog"* Elvis later made famous) deeply influenced him. In fact, many Black artists respected Elvis for his vocal talent and his acknowledgment of Black roots in his work. B.B. King once said, *"Elvis had an influence on everybody with his musical approach. He broke the ice for all of us."*

Yet this relationship was not without tension. While Black artists laid the foundation for rock and roll, it was

Elvis—a white man—who reaped the commercial benefits. He topped charts that Black artists were barred from. Radio stations that wouldn't play Chuck Berry or Little Richard eagerly broadcast Presley.

This paradox—respect for his musical tribute and resentment at the inequality—defines much of the African American perspective on Elvis.

## Religious Groups: Both Condemned and Celebrated

Elvis' early performances sparked outrage from some religious and conservative circles. Baptist ministers, Catholic commentators, and community leaders labeled his stage movements "lewd" and his music "devilish." Pastors warned from the pulpit that rock 'n' roll, especially Presley's variety, would lead youth to sin, rebellion, and moral decay.

But the story didn't end there. Elvis had a profound spiritual side. His mother Gladys raised him in a Pentecostal church, and gospel music remained a cornerstone of his life and career. Some of his most passionate performances were not rock hits but gospel recordings like *"Peace in the Valley"*, *"How Great Thou Art"*, and *"He Touched Me."* He won three Grammy Awards, and all were for gospel recordings.

This contrast between secular performer and spiritual seeker made Elvis a symbol of both temptation and redemption, depending on one's point of view.

## The Working Class: One of Their Own

Elvis never shed the image of a humble boy from Tupelo, Mississippi. Raised in poverty, living in public housing, and working odd jobs before his breakthrough, he became a symbol of the American Dream for the working class.

Factory workers, truck drivers, mechanics, waitresses— they saw themselves in Elvis. He didn't talk like the elite or act like the privileged. He stayed close to his roots, famously buying homes and cars for his family and friends. One of his closest confidantes, Jerry Schilling, once remarked, *"He never forgot where he came from— that's why the people loved him."*

When Elvis returned to perform in Las Vegas in the 1970s, his shows were filled with working-class fans, many of whom had followed his career since the beginning. They weren't just coming to hear the music— they were coming to support one of their own who made it big.

## Women: Fan Frenzy, But Also Emotional Connection

Elvis was an early icon of mass female fandom. His looks, voice, and vulnerability made him a sensation. His concerts sparked screaming frenzies, fainting fans, and in some cases, security interventions. But it would be a mistake to dismiss this reaction as simple infatuation.

At a time when mainstream male artists were stoic and controlled, Elvis expressed pain, longing, and affection through his songs. Ballads like *"Love Me Tender"*, *"Are You Lonesome Tonight?"*, and *"Can't Help Falling in Love"* gave voice to deep emotional currents. For many women, this was refreshing—and empowering.

Even in a society that tried to repress women's sexuality, Elvis allowed emotional openness and romantic vulnerability to become part of mainstream music. Many women saw in him a rare blend of strength and sensitivity.

## International Audiences: Elvis the Global Star

Elvis' impact was not confined to American borders. His records were distributed in dozens of countries, and his fame spread rapidly. In Germany, where he served in the U.S. Army from 1958 to 1960, he won over locals with his humility and charm. He recorded songs in German and developed friendships with local musicians.

In the United Kingdom, future rock stars like John Lennon and Mick Jagger described seeing Elvis as a transformative moment. Lennon said, *"Before Elvis, there was nothing."* In Japan, South Africa, and South America, Elvis represented the allure of Western freedom and musical innovation. He became a cultural export, a soft-power ambassador through the universal language of music.

Even in nations that viewed America with skepticism, Elvis was embraced as a purely musical icon—someone whose voice transcended politics.

## Conclusion: One Voice, Many Echoes

Elvis Presley's music was a prism: when you looked through it, different truths emerged for different people. He was a teen icon, a racial flashpoint, a spiritual enigma, a working-class hero, a symbol of female awakening, and a global ambassador. Few figures in modern history have managed to connect so many disparate groups—sometimes uniting them, sometimes dividing them, but always sparking emotion.

His legacy is complicated, as all major legacies are. But in understanding how Elvis affected different groups, we come to see the profound ability of music to reflect, shape, and challenge the social currents of its time.

# Chapter 23: The Future of Music and Its Benefits

As technology advances and society evolves, the role of music in our lives continues to expand and transform. The future of music holds exciting possibilities that promise to deepen and broaden its hidden benefits, enhancing mental health, education, creativity, social connection, and beyond. Understanding these emerging trends helps us appreciate how music will remain a vital, dynamic force in human culture and well-being.

One of the most significant changes shaping music's future is the integration of digital technology and artificial intelligence. Streaming platforms, smart devices, and AI-generated compositions are making music more accessible and personalized than before. Listeners can now curate individualized soundscapes tailored to their moods, activities, and health needs. This personalization opens new doors for music's therapeutic applications, allowing real-time adjustments that optimize relaxation, focus, or motivation.

Virtual and augmented reality technologies promise to revolutionize music experiences by creating immersive environments where people can interact with music in multisensory ways. Imagine attending a concert from your living room with 360-degree visuals and surround sound or collaborating with musicians worldwide in virtual studios. These innovations will enhance social bonding and creativity, breaking down physical and cultural barriers.

The future also holds promise for expanding music therapy and its applications. Advances in neuroscience and biofeedback technology enable more precise understanding of how music affects the brain and body. This knowledge will allow therapists to design highly customized interventions for conditions ranging from neurological disorders to mental health challenges. Integrating music therapy with other digital health tools will improve patient outcomes and accessibility.

In education, technology will continue to make music learning more interactive and inclusive. Online platforms, apps, and AI tutors offer personalized instruction that adapts to learners' pace and style. This democratization of music education will empower more people to develop musical skills and enjoy its cognitive and emotional benefits, regardless of geographic or socioeconomic barriers.

Socially, music's role as a connector will grow stronger through digital communities and collaborative platforms. People from diverse backgrounds can share music, co-create, and support each other, fostering global understanding and empathy. Music's capacity to unite despite differences will be more vital than ever in an increasingly interconnected yet divided world.

Sustainability and ethical considerations are also shaping music's future. Artists, producers, and audiences are becoming more aware of the environmental impact of music production and live events, prompting innovations in eco-friendly practices. Moreover, the music industry is grappling with issues of equity, representation, and fair compensation, seeking to create a more inclusive and just ecosystem.

Importantly, the core essence of music—as a source of joy, healing, expression, and connection—will remain unchanged. While the mediums and methods evolve, the fundamental human need for music's emotional and social nourishment endures. As we embrace new technologies and opportunities, we must also honor the timeless power of music to touch the soul.

In conclusion, the future of music is bright and full of potential. By harnessing technological innovations, expanding therapeutic and educational uses, and nurturing its social and cultural significance, music will continue to enrich lives in profound and unexpected ways. Embracing this future invites us all to participate in the ongoing story of music's remarkable benefits.

# Chapter 24: Conclusion: The Quiet Power That Changes Everything

Music is more than sound. It is more than art. It is more than entertainment. Music is one of humanity's oldest and most enduring tools for healing, learning, connecting, and transforming. And yet, for all its presence in our daily lives, its benefits often remain quietly hidden—working beneath the surface to shape our minds, hearts, and communities.

Throughout this book, we have pulled back the curtain on music's unseen power. We have walked through hospital rooms where music eased the pain of recovery. We've stepped into classrooms where melody helped unlock learning. We've stood beside people living with memory loss who, upon hearing a familiar tune, smiled with recognition for the first time in weeks. And we've seen how music gave strength to individuals battling anxiety, depression, trauma, and loneliness.

# A Universal Language with Infinite Dialects

Music crosses boundaries that words cannot. It transcends language, nationality, and religion. A drumbeat in the Congo speaks to a violinist in Vienna. A folk song from Appalachia resonates in the streets of Seoul. Whether it's gospel in a small-town church, techno in a city club, or lullabies sung in whispered tones, music is universal—but never impersonal. Each song is a fingerprint of culture and emotion. Each rhythm carries a heartbeat of belonging.

In every country, in every generation, music has been used to protest injustice, mourn loss, celebrate victory, and express the inexpressible. It does not require translation. It only asks to be heard.

# Personal Transformation, One Note at a Time

Perhaps the most surprising realization is that you don't need to be a musician to benefit deeply from music. You don't need a perfect ear, a trained voice, or a room full of instruments. Music meets you wherever you are.

Feeling discouraged? A song can lift your mood. Feeling lost? Lyrics can help you feel seen. Feeling overwhelmed? A soft instrumental can calm your nervous system.

Creating music—whether through humming, drumming, or composing—can deepen this transformation. Even brief, informal musical moments can reduce stress, increase focus, or invite creativity. It's not about performance. It's about participation. Engaging with music invites a dialogue between your inner world and the outer world.

## Music as a Lifelong Ally

From infancy to old age, music is always available to us. Babies are soothed by lullabies long before they can understand language. Teenagers often turn to music to define their identity. Adults rely on it to motivate, to reflect, to escape. And in our later years, music often becomes a companion to memory and meaning.

Studies have shown that individuals with dementia can often recall and respond to songs long after speech and recognition have faded. Why? Because music reaches parts of the brain that other functions cannot. It anchors us. It reminds us. It holds us.

## The Emotional Truth of Music

At its core, music is a truth-teller. It brings us face-to-face with our own feelings—sometimes in ways we didn't expect. A song can transport you back in time in a single note. It can help you cry when you've been holding back. It can help you dance when you didn't know you had the energy. It can say what you couldn't put into words.

Even silence becomes sacred when followed by a moving piece of music. In that quiet moment after the last note fades, we feel its echo—not just in our ears, but in our spirit.

# A Call to Listen—And to Use Music Intentionally

As you finish this book, consider not only what music has meant to you—but what it could mean if used more intentionally.

- Could starting your day with music set a more positive tone?
- Could making a playlist of calming songs help with sleep or anxiety?
- Could singing with your children deepen connection?
- Could learning an instrument at any age stimulate new growth and joy?

Music is not just for special occasions. It's not just for background noise. It's a living, breathing resource for emotional, cognitive, and social well-being. And it's entirely within your reach.

## Final Thoughts: Your Life, Scored in Sound

The hidden benefits of music are not truly hidden. They are waiting—beneath each chord, behind every lyric, inside every rhythm. Whether you seek healing, clarity, connection, or joy, music is already offering you a path. You only need to listen.

So, tune in.

To your heart.
To your mind.
To the music all around you.

Let music become more than something you hear—let it become something you live by. Because your life deserves a soundtrack that uplifts, heals, and empowers you—one note at a time.

# Additional Reading Choices

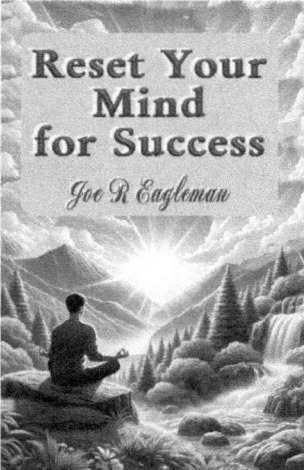

# ABOUT THE AUTHOR

Joe R. Eagleman (1936- ) was born on a farm near West Plains Missouri. He received the PhD from the University of Missouri in 1963 and was a professor at the University of Kansas for 39 years. He taught thousands of students about Atmospheric Science through his courses there and many thousands more  through four different textbooks used by over a hundred universities over a span of several decades. He directed a successful experiment on Skylab, funded by NASA, and invented a tornado in his laboratory that was used by Universal Studios for a 50 ft. tornado attraction in the Twister Building in Orlando Florida for several decades. It can still be seer. at the Exploratorium in San Francisco.

He is the author of a technical book on severe thunderstorms that includes his tornado safety research which resulted in changes that were adopted nationally. His autobiography, *Name Your Price*, tells of his early life on a farm where he was the 11th of 12 children. It includes his work as a scientist as well as a number of unusual hobbies including those as an artist, musician, luthier, marksman, taxidermist, world traveler and other endeavors.

He has also published his second autobiography, *Monumental Moments*, that captures the most significant times of his life and *Eagleman Stories* that contains stories from his life as well as his 11 siblings and his parents.

Since his retirement he has published numerous books and recorded four albums of original music. For more information see http://www.JoeEagleman.com.